We March for You

Messages to Girls from the Women's Marches

Written by Penny McDonald   Illustrated by Raquel Mora Vega

On January 21, 2017, we marched. We marched all over the world, in great big cities and in tiny towns.

We marched with our handmade signs in many languages.

We marched for ourselves.
We marched for our families.
We marched for our friends.

But most of all we marched for you, girls now, women in the future. We marched for you, daughters, granddaughters, students, girls we do not know.

Whenever we march, we march forward, always forward.

4

"The future depends entirely on what each of us does every day; a movement is only people moving."

Gloria Steinem

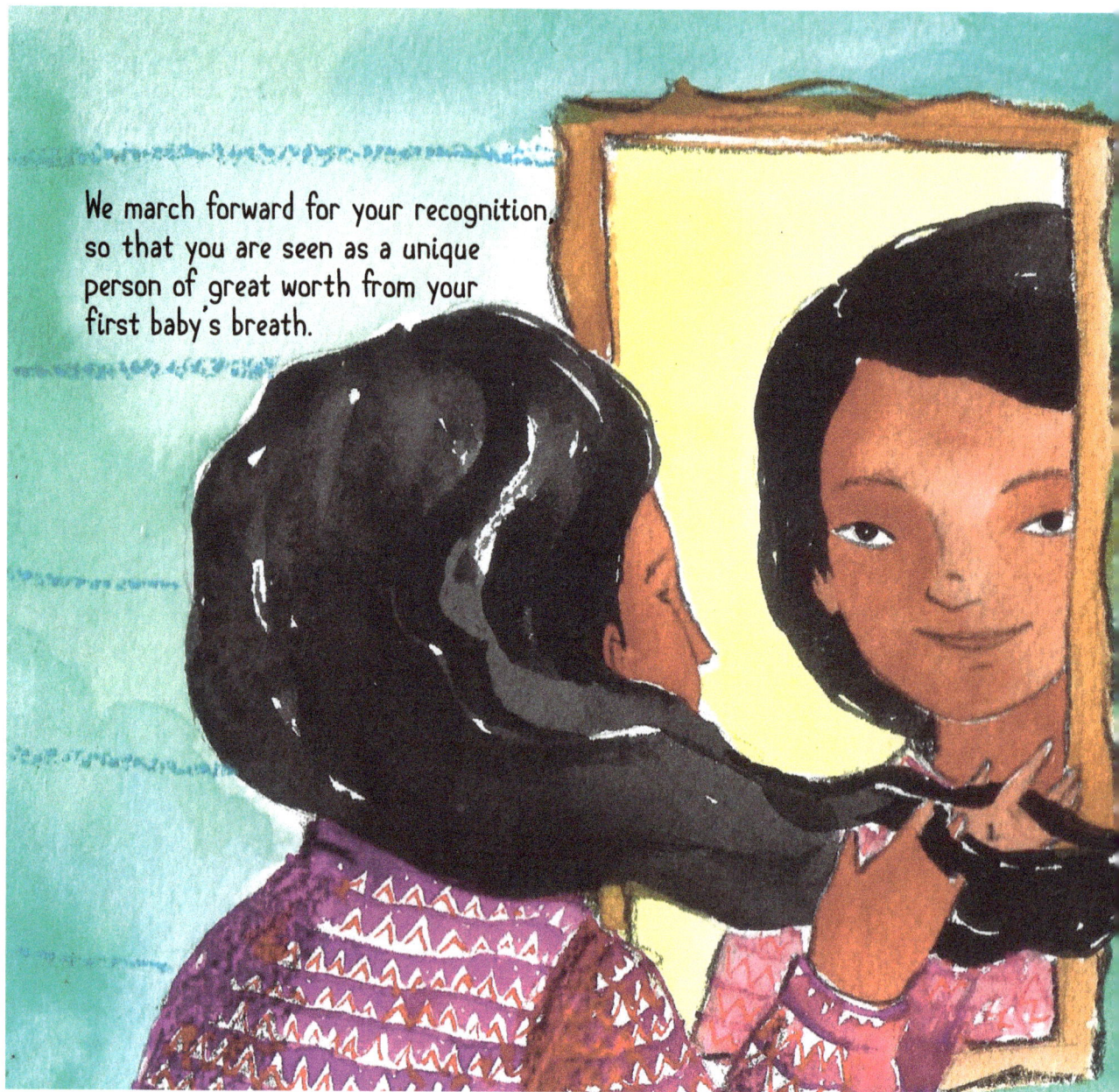

We march forward for your recognition,
so that you are seen as a unique
person of great worth from your
first baby's breath.

6

"If it is true that the full humanity of women is not our culture, then we can and must make it our culture."

Chimamanda Ngozi Adichie

We march forward for your security, for a life free from danger, for comforting shelter and nutritious food.

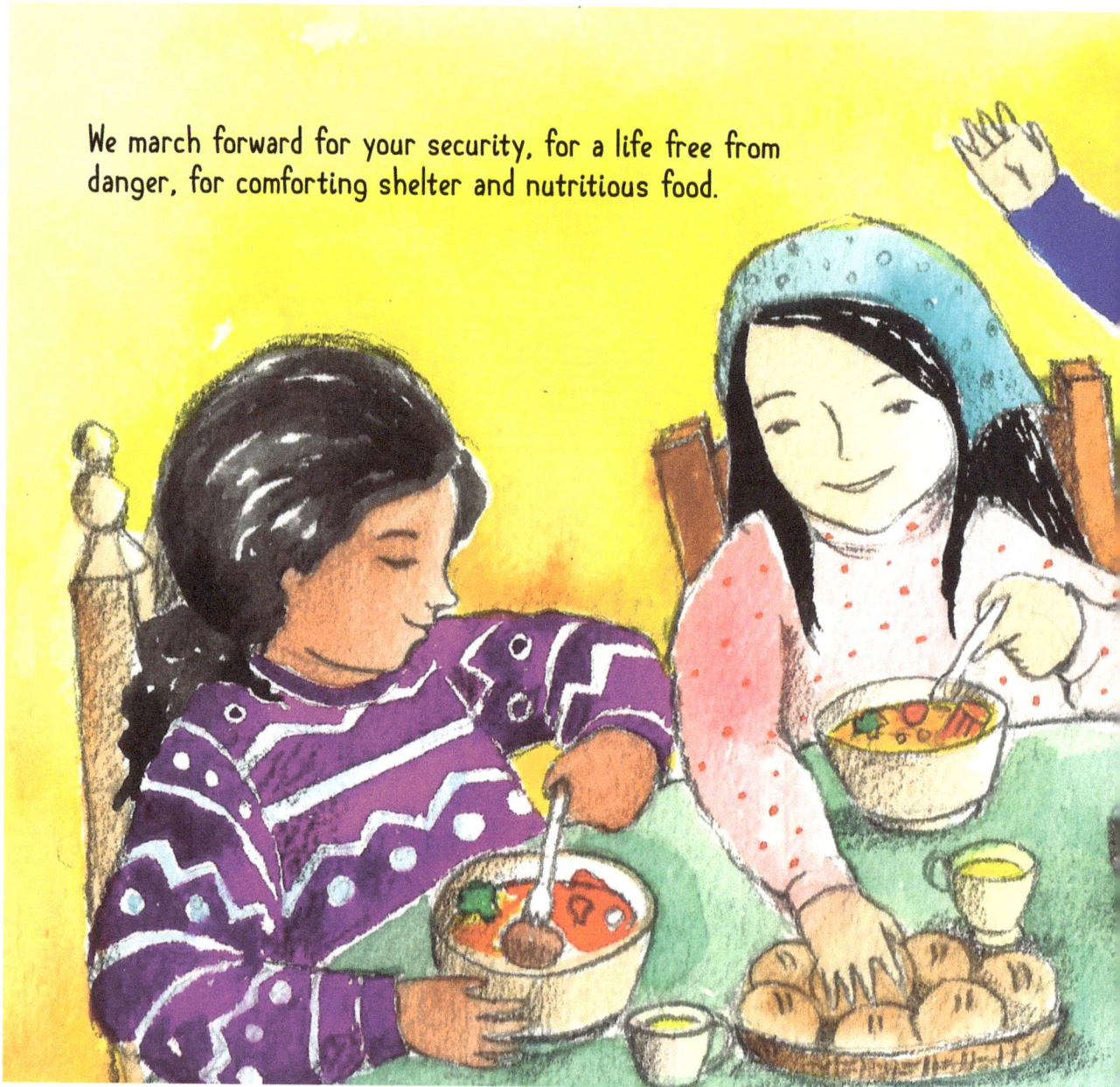

8

"Rock bottom became the solid foundation on which I rebuilt my life."
J.K. Rowling

We march forward for your health
—body and mind— for skilled
doctors, protection from disease,
and the medicines to keep you well.

"It is not easy to
be a pioneer — but,
oh, it is fascinating!

I would not trade
one moment, even
the worst moment,
for all the riches in
the world."

Dr. Elizabeth
Blackwell

11

We march forward for all the possibilities of love in your life.

12

"Love recognizes no barriers. It jumps hurdles, leaps fences, penetrates walls to arrive at its destination full of hope."

Maya Angelou

We march forward for your education, for schooling that takes all the potential of your mind both far and wide.

"Girls should never be afraid to be smart."

Emma Watson

We march forward for respect of your abilities and challenges — and your respect for them in others.

"Autism is part of who I am."
Temple Grandin

17

We march forward for your life's purpose,
whatever passion draws you — sometimes
home, sometimes career, sometimes a special
cause, sometimes all at once.

"I have no dress except the one I wear every day. If you are going to be kind enough to give me one, please let it be practical and dark so that I can put it on afterwards to go to the laboratory."

Marie Curie

We march forward for your freedom to make choices, about your life and how you live it.

"It is very important to know who you are. To make decisions. To show who you are."
Malala

21

We march forward for your support by men and of men.

"Let's be very clear: Strong men...don't need to put women down to make themselves feel powerful. People who are truly strong lift others up."

Michelle Obama

23

We march forward for your
natural world, clean air and
water, protection of its
wonders and beauties.

24

"The tree I had in the garden as a child, my beech tree, I used to Iclimb up there and spend hours.

I took my homework up there, my books, I went up there if I was sad, and it just felt very good to be up there among the green leaves and the birds and the sky."

Jane Goodall

25

We march forward for your open arms to a world of differences, that you both welcome others and see beyond your own home.

26

"This is our cry. This is our prayer: peace in the world."

Sadako Sasaki
Monument in Hiroshima

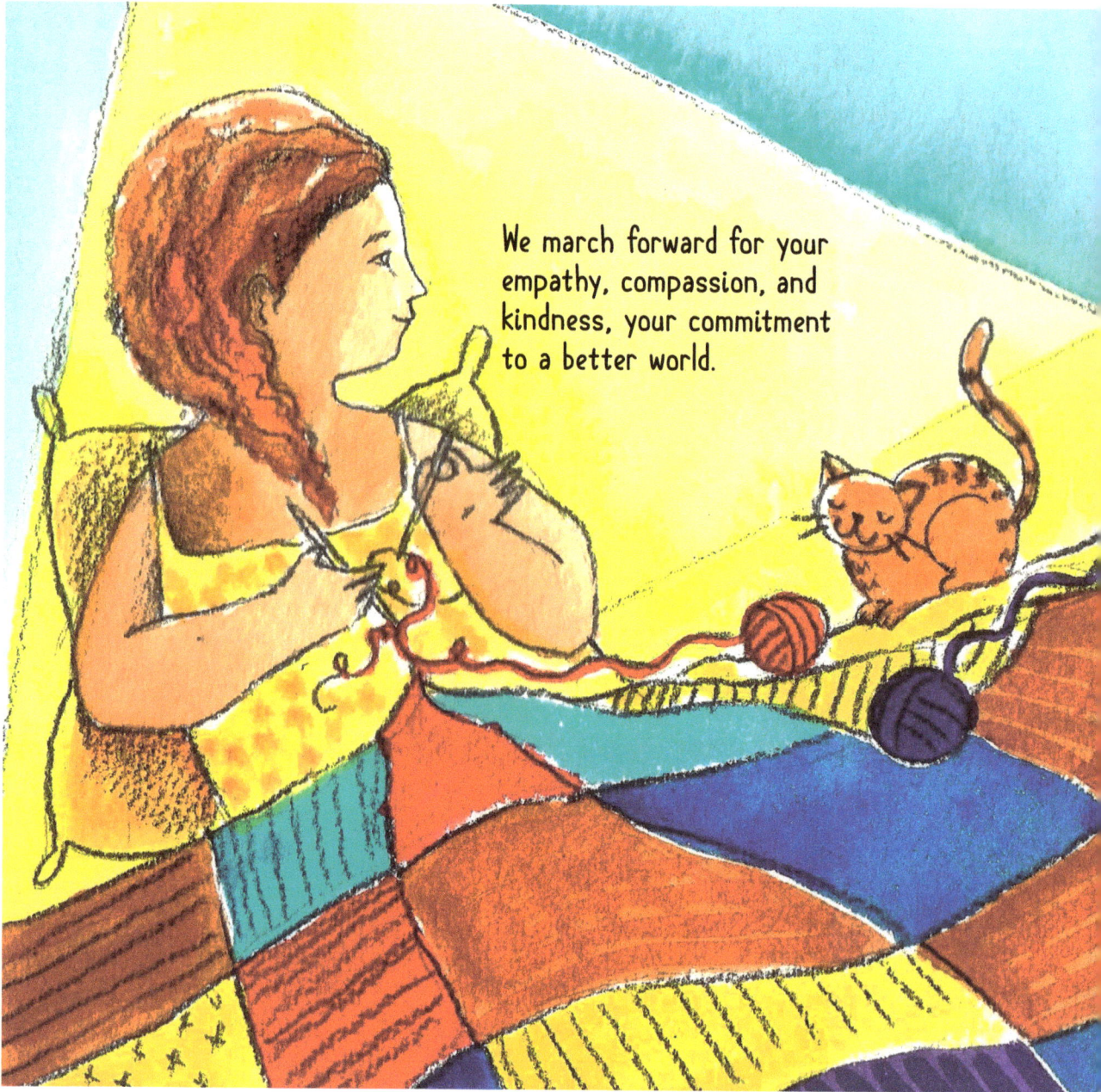

We march forward for your empathy, compassion, and kindness, your commitment to a better world.

28

"People are just people, and all
have faults and shortcomings,
but all of us are born with
a basic goodness."
Anne Frank

29

We march forward for your pride in who you are and where you come from, your strength in even nearly unimaginable hardship.

"I am as strong as any man that is now."
Sojourner Truth

We march forward for your connection to your own soul
and to the spirit of others through art, music, books.

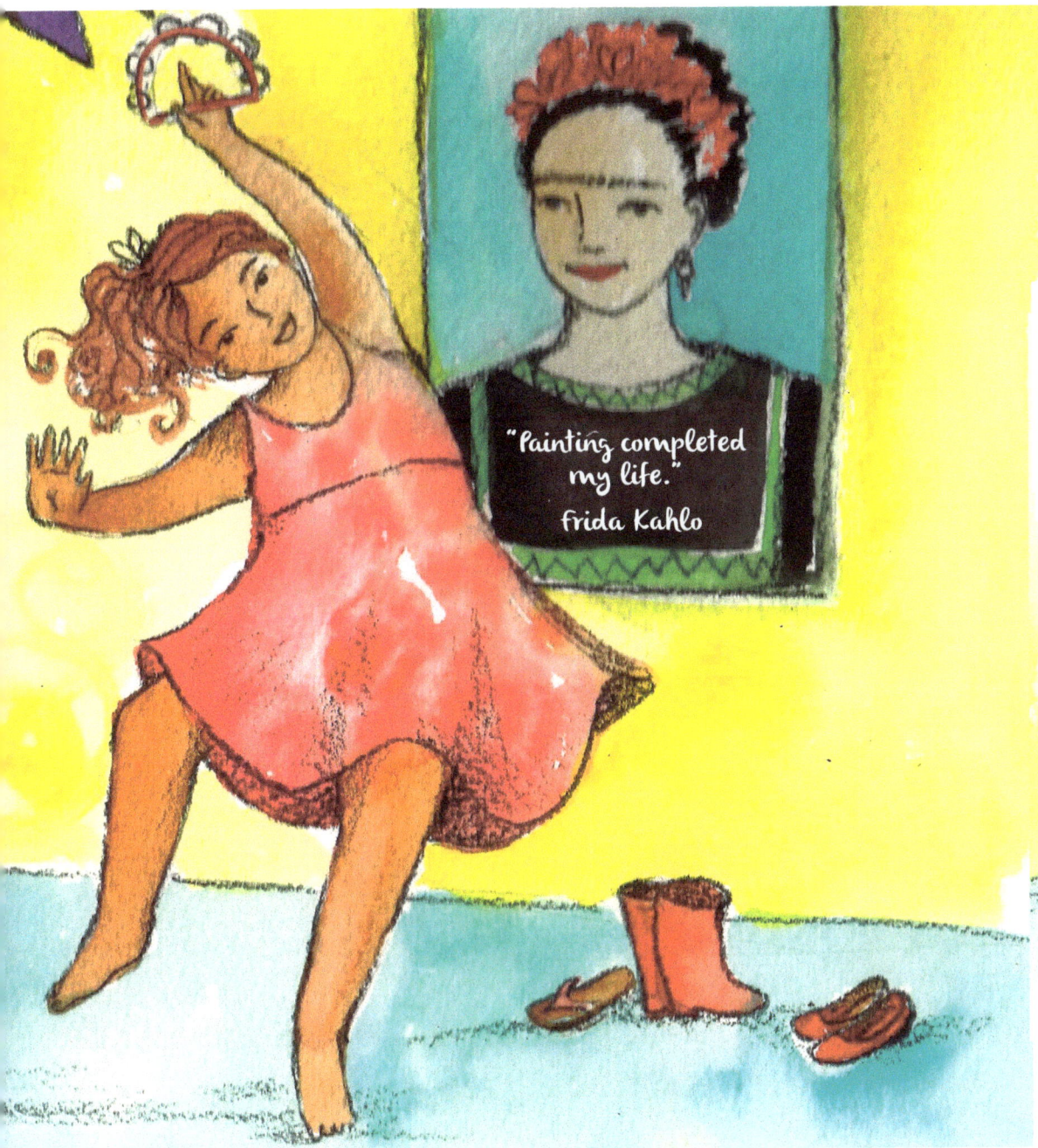

"Painting completed my life."

Frida Kahlo

We march forward for your confidence and daring to do what is right, to fight what is wrong.

"I have learned over the years that when one's mind is made up, this diminishes fear;

knowing what must be done does away with fear."
Rosa Parks

On January 21, 2017, we marched
forward, all over the world, for you.

We marched in the footsteps of other women
throughout history and around the globe.

You are such a precious person, and your life will move us forward too. You can march forward for yourself, your friends, your own daughters and granddaughters, girls you do not know.

Always forward, never back – no, never back.

"The young women of today, free to study, to speak, to write, to choose their occupation, should remember that every inch of this freedom was bought for them at a great price." Abigail Scott Duniway

39

Author's Note

"Women are the largest untapped reservoir of talent in the world."

Hillary Clinton

Dear Readers,

My name is Penny Mc Donald, and I am the Author. I'm 72 years old and live in the United States. I wrote this book, because I am a Feminist who wants a good life for every girl like you.

When I was a girl, there were many differences in opportunities. I heard Nos. No, don't get good grades; boys don't like smart girls. No, we won't even notice your math abilities, because girls don't become mathematicians, scientists, engineers. Men are mathematicians, scientists, engineers. No, don't dare to go to law school. Men are lawyers. You can be a teacher, but No, not a principal. Men are principals.

That was my story. Each woman has her own. And life is very much more difficult, if born to a less loving family, born years before, born a person of color, born poor, born in countries with more Nos.

So many wonderful changes in my lifetime! Our rights as women must never regress. Our work is not done; the things we march for are not true-- not yet, not for all of us. I want you valued equally with boys and men: equal respect, equal rights, and equal pay. Equality is not only good for you, but also for your country, our whole world.

That is why we march for you,

Penny Mc Donald

(By the way, I did become a school principal. I didn't take no for an answer!)

Illustrator's Note

"Yo creo en el Dios de la compasión, y cada vez creo más en el Dios que también es mujer, que también es femenino…"

"I believe in the God of compassion and, more and more, I believe in the God who is also a woman, who is also feminine…"

María López Vigil

Dear Readers,

My name is Raquel Mora Vega, and I am the illustrator of this book. I'm 33 years old and live in Costa Rica. I illustrated this book because Penny is my good friend and we marched so many times in our countries where there are different forms of inequality and violence against women.

I tried to draw and paint with my watercolors the words that Penny wrote for you, and I was always imagining and feeling the world that I dream: a world with good food, education, art, love, friendship, rights, respect, and a dignified life for every girl and woman everywhere and every day.

I feel very happy because I can share with you what these words mean for me through my illustrations. It could mean something different for you. Maybe you also could draw the reasons why the women and girls keep marching.

Let´s keep dreaming and creating the world we want and deserve.

Raquel Mora Vega

Questions for discussion and writing

- Why do you think the author wrote a book especially for girls? Do you think boys should read it too? Why?

- In a picture book like this, of course, the words send messages to the reader, but so does the art. What messages do you see in Raquel's illustrations?

- Penny says she is a Feminist. What is a Feminist? Pick out any other vocabulary on these pages that you would like to understand better.

- Ask your family, a teacher, the librarian: How was life different for girls when you were growing up? And how might you like it to be different in the future for girls like me?

- Choose a quote that interests you. What do you know about the person speaking?

- What other women and girls do you admire? What messages do you think they would have for girls?

- Some of the females quoted are quite young. As a young girl, how do you think you can make the world better?

- Ten years from now, what would you like to be doing with your life? How about later in your life, what dreams do you have?

42

Bibliography

A sampling of related BOOKS, for various ages, babies to Nanas…

Brantz, L. (2017). Feminist baby. Los Angeles, CA: Disney-Hyperion.

Clinton, C. (2015). It's your world: Get informed, get inspired & get going. New York, NY: Philomel Books.

Favilli, E. & Cavallo, F. (2016). Good night stories for rebel girls: 100 stories of extraordinary women. [Venice, CA]: Timbuktu Labs.

Frank, A., & Frank, O., & Pressler, M. (Eds.). (1996). The diary of a young girl: The definitive edition (S. Massotty, Trans.). New York, NY: Anchor Books.

Giovanni, N. (2005). Rosa. New York, NY: Holt.

Ignotofsky, R. (2016). Women in science: 50 fearless pioneers who changed the world. Berkeley, CA: Ten Speed Press.

Langston-George, R. (2016). For the right to learn: Malala Yousafzai's story. North Mankato, MN: Capstone Press.

Levinson, C. (2017). The youngest marcher: The story of Audrey Faye Hendricks, a young civil rights activist. New York, NY: Atheneum Books for Young Readers.

O' Leary, C. & Spring, J. (2016). Dead feminists: Historical heroines in living color. Seattle, WA: Sasquatch Books.

Sanna, F. (2016). The journey. London, England: Flying Eye Books.

Stone, T. (2008). Elizabeth leads the way: Elizabeth Cady Stanton and the right to vote. New York, NY: Holt.

And a sampling of WEBSITES for girls and the adults who help them learn more about women and their history…

Feminism: www.cliohistory.org/click

The History Channel: www.history.com/topics/womens-history

National Women's History Museum: www.nwhm.org

Notable people: www.biography.com

Teaching Tolerance: www.tolerance.org

43

Thank You

A special abrazo, or hug, for Marisa Baragli Bevington, who said, "Write, Penny." She was copied on every single email between Raquel and me, for any needed translation — and for her artist's eye as well. I was so grateful for this willingness to help us whether she was volunteering at Chaco National Park or traveling in Europe or Mexico.

On January 21, 2017, Marisa marched in my hometown of Portland, Oregon, in the rain. However, she first saw the power in women marching in her native Argentina, where women wearing white kerchiefs with the names of their missing children march every Thursday. This started in the 1970s to bravely protest "disappearances" during government dictatorship. Still today Las Madres y Abuelas de la Plaza de Mayo (the Mothers and Grandmothers of the Plaza de Mayo) march every Thursday to express their ongoing commitment to finding their children.

Abrazos as well to those who helped me in so many other ways: Karen Graham, Michele Stemler, Marilyn McDonald; Pat Haley and Kristie Skovgaard, Judith Downs and Michael Donovan, and all housesit locations providing writing support and tranquility; Pat Schmuck; Simon Calcavecchia; Neale Inahara and Guadalupe Leon; Family: Ava, Katie, and Aidan plus Jenn and Dale, Mike and Linda; staff in Oregon and Washington cafes; librarians in Portland; Pantsuit Nation and We March for Our Lives; photographer Molly Adams and MS. Magazine; book designer Cheryl McLean; United States Holocaust Memorial Museum; Oregon-Costa Rica Partners; Starseed Foundation; Inkwater Press.

www.ingramcontent.com/pod-product-compliance
Lightning Source LLC
Chambersburg PA
CBHW040245100426
42811CB00011B/1160